Tension Techniques Guide

Keep Your Readers Hooked, Scene by Scene

Connie Bauldree
Author by Design

Tension Techniques Guide: Keep Your Readers Hooked, Scene by Scene

Published by BaulConn Publishing
www.authorbydesign.co www.writersblockboxes.com

Introduction

Tension is the lifeblood of every story. Whether you're writing nail-biting suspense or a quiet, emotional journey. It's that underlying current of uncertainty, anticipation, or unease that makes readers lean in, hold their breath, and keep flipping pages long after midnight.

But tension isn't just for thrillers. It's woven into every genre and every scene, from a whispered secret in a romance to the ticking clock of a heist or the silent dread before a horror reveal. Great tension keeps your characters, and your readers, on edge, always wondering what will happen next.

This guide is packed with practical, hands-on techniques to help you:

- Create anticipation and raise stakes, even in small moments
- Use silence, subtext, and setting to make scenes crackle
- Build tension line by line, not just in big plot twists
- Diagnose and fix scenes that fall flat or lose momentum

Each section includes clear explanations, original examples, and workbook prompts to help you practice and apply each skill directly to your own story. Whether you're plotting, drafting, or revising, these tools will help you add the kind of tension that keeps your readers hooked from the first sentence to the final page.

Ready to turn up the heat in your writing? Let's dive in.

Withholding Information & Unanswered Questions

Tension is born from uncertainty. When you withhold information, whether it's a secret, a motive, or the outcome of a crucial decision, you create a gap between what the reader knows and what the characters know. This gap keeps your audience leaning forward, hungry for answers.

Techniques in Action

1. Dramatic Irony (Reader Knows More):

In a thriller, the reader sees the villain plant a bomb under the table. The protagonist sits down for lunch, unaware. Every detail of the scene is charged with tension because the audience is waiting for disaster.

2. Character Secrets (Character Knows More):

In a romance, one lover hides a painful secret from the other. Every conversation, every hesitation, is colored by what's left unsaid. The tension grows as the truth threatens to come out.

3. Unanswered Questions (Everyone's in the Dark):

End a scene with a mystery: "What's in the box?" "Who left the message?" "Will she say yes?" Each question is a hook that keeps readers engaged.

4. Misdirection and Red Herrings:

In mysteries, authors often plant false clues or distract the reader's attention, making the real answer more satisfying when it finally arrives.

Genre Applications

- **Thriller:** Secrets about identity, hidden threats, or ticking bombs.
- **Romance:** Unspoken feelings, past relationships, or future plans.

- **Fantasy:** Mysterious prophecies, hidden powers, or concealed lineages.
- **Literary:** Family secrets, personal regrets, or unspoken trauma.

Pro Tips & Troubleshooting

Pro Tip: *Withhold just enough. Give readers clues so they can anticipate, but not predict, the outcome.*

Troubleshooting:

- If readers are confused, clarify what's being withheld and why.
- If tension drops, ask: Did I reveal the answer too soon? Can I delay the reveal, or add a new question?

Mini Checklist

- ☐ Is there at least one secret, question, or mystery driving your story forward?
- ☐ Have you dropped subtle clues or hints for attentive readers?
- ☐ Does every reveal create new questions or complications?

Advanced Applications

- **Layered Secrets:** Multiple characters each hide something, creating a web of tension.
- **Delayed Payoff:** Tease a secret in Chapter 1, but don't reveal it until much later. Keep the question alive through callbacks and hints.
- **Combining Techniques:** Withhold information while also adding a ticking clock or contradictory goals for maximum tension.

Common Problems

Q: What if readers get frustrated?

A: Make sure the payoff is worth the wait. Don't withhold just for the sake of it. Give them a satisfying answer or twist.

Q: How do I avoid info-dumping when I finally reveal the answer?

A: Show the consequences of the reveal through action and reaction, not just exposition.

Try This

- Rewrite a key scene in your story so that a crucial detail is withheld. How does it change the scene's energy?
- List three unanswered questions in your current draft. How can you delay the answers for more tension?

Ticking Clocks & Time Pressure

Nothing raises tension faster than a deadline. When characters are racing against the clock, whether it's a literal timer, a looming event, or a personal deadline, every decision carries extra weight. Time pressure forces characters to act, make mistakes, and reveal their true priorities.

Techniques in Action

1. Literal Ticking Clocks:
- A bomb set to go off in ten minutes.
- A race to rescue someone before sunrise.
- A courtroom drama where the verdict is due by noon.

2. Looming Events:
- The wedding starts in one hour, but the ring is missing.
- The villain's plan will unfold at midnight.
- A character must confess the truth before their partner leaves town.

3. Personal Deadlines:
- A protagonist has one week to save their business.
- A student must finish a project before graduation.
- A character's health is failing and they have limited time to make amends.

4. Escalating Time Pressure:
- The deadline keeps moving closer, or unexpected obstacles make the original time frame impossible.

Genre Applications
- **Thriller:** Bombs, chases, or investigations with strict time limits.
- **Romance:** A love confession must happen

before someone leaves.

- **Fantasy/Sci-Fi:** Prophecies or cosmic events on a set timeline.
- **Mystery:** A detective must solve the case before another crime occurs.

Pro Tips & Troubleshooting

Pro Tip: *Let the characters and reader feel the countdown. Use reminders in dialogue, scene breaks, or physical cues (clocks, alarms, fading light).*

Troubleshooting:

- If the time pressure feels artificial, tie it to something real and urgent for the character.
- If scenes drag, remind readers of the deadline to keep tension high.

Mini Checklist

- ☐ Is there a clear, urgent deadline driving the action?
- ☐ Do characters make riskier choices as time runs out?
- ☐ Are there reminders of time passing throughout the scene or chapter?
- ☐ Does the deadline escalate or change unexpectedly?

Advanced Applications

- **Multiple Clocks:** Different characters have different deadlines, causing conflict.
- **False Deadline:** The clock runs out, but the real crisis is just beginning.
- **Countdown Structure:** Open each chapter with a time marker ("12 hours to go...").

Common Problems

Q: What if my story feels rushed?
A: Balance fast-paced scenes with brief pauses for

reflection. Use time pressure to heighten key moments, not every scene.

Q: How do I avoid "deadline fatigue"?
A: Vary the type and intensity of time pressure. Not every moment needs a ticking clock, but the biggest stakes should always feel urgent.

Try This

- Take a scene with low energy and add a time limit. How do your characters' choices change?
- Brainstorm three ways a looming deadline could force your protagonist into action—or into making a mistake they wouldn't otherwise make.

Subtext, Silence, and Body Language

Tension isn't always about what's said. It's often about what's left unsaid. Subtext, silence, and body language create emotional friction beneath the surface of dialogue and action. When characters dodge questions, avoid eye contact, or communicate with a look, readers sense that more is happening than meets the eye. This "between the lines" tension is irresistible and universal.

Techniques in Action

1. Subtext in Dialogue:
- Characters say one thing but mean another ("I'm fine," when they're clearly not).
- The real issue is never named, but every word is loaded with hidden meaning.
  Example: Two ex-lovers talk about the weather while avoiding the real reason for their breakup.

2. Strategic Silence:
- Pauses, unfinished sentences, or awkward silences heighten discomfort.
- A character's refusal to answer a question creates more tension than any argument.
  Example: In a family dinner scene, a single unanswered question hangs in the air, making everyone uneasy.

3. Body Language:
- Fidgeting, crossed arms, averted eyes, clenched jaws, all reveal inner conflict.
- Physical distance or proximity signals intimacy, threat, or avoidance.
  Example: A detective leans in, suspect leans back - their bodies "argue" before their words do.

4. Layering Subtext and Action:

- What the character does contradicts what they say.
  Example: "I trust you," she says, but she locks the door behind him.

Genre Applications

- **Romance:** Longing glances, almost-touches, conversations loaded with what isn't said.
- **Thriller/Mystery:** Interrogations where suspects dodge, deflect, and sweat.
- **Contemporary/Literary:** Family gatherings, breakups, or reunions where silence says it all.
- **Fantasy/Sci-Fi:** Negotiations between enemies, coded gestures in forbidden settings.

Pro Tips & Troubleshooting

Pro Tip: Read your dialogue out loud. If every character always says exactly what they mean, layer in subtext or a moment of silence.

Troubleshooting:

- If a scene feels flat, add a secret or a lie, then have the character try to hide it with words or actions.
- If dialogue is too on-the-nose, rewrite with more implication and less explanation.

Mini Checklist

- ☐ Do your characters ever say one thing but mean another?
- ☐ Are there moments where silence or a pause increases tension?
- ☐ Does body language reveal what dialogue conceals?
- ☐ Are important emotions or stakes hidden beneath the surface?

Advanced Applications

- **Power Plays:** Use silence or stillness as a way for one character to control the scene.
- **Misdirection:** Let a character's words soothe while their body signals danger.
- **Escalation:** Build a scene where tension rises with every unspoken word or gesture, then finally explodes.

Common Problems

Q: What if readers miss the subtext?
A: Use physical cues (blushing, sweating, shifting in a seat) to hint at what's really going on.

Q: How do I keep silence from stalling the scene?
A: Make sure the silence is loaded with secrets, anticipation, or threat. Use action or inner monologue to keep momentum.

Try This

- Rewrite a scene's dialogue so that the real conflict is never named. Let body language and silence do the work.
- Watch a favorite movie scene on mute. What tension do you pick up from the actors' faces, gestures, and pauses? Try to capture that in your writing.

Contradictory Goals & Shifting Power

Tension skyrockets when two or more characters want different things at the same time and neither is willing to back down. These contradictory goals create friction, drive scenes forward, and keep readers on edge. When the balance of power shifts (even subtly), every line and action becomes charged with possibility and risk.

Techniques in Action

1. Direct Opposition:

- Two characters argue, negotiate, or compete, each with a clear, opposing goal.
  Example: A detective wants a confession; the suspect wants to escape blame.

2. Hidden Agendas:

- One or more characters have secret motives or goals that aren't revealed until later.
  Example: In a workplace, two employees vie for the same promotion. One plays fair, the other sabotages.

3. Emotional Stakes:

- Contradictory goals aren't always about winning or losing; sometimes, it's about love, trust, or forgiveness.
  Example: One partner wants to talk about a problem, the other wants to avoid conflict.

4. Power Shifts:

- The upper hand changes during the scene through a reveal, a threat, or a clever move.
  Example: In a debate, one character starts in control, but a new piece of information turns the tables.

Genre Applications

- **Thriller:** Interrogations, hostage negotiations, or cat-and-mouse chases.
- **Romance:** Lovers with clashing dreams, breakups, or make-or-break ultimatums.
- **Fantasy/Sci-Fi:** Council meetings, magical duels, or battles for leadership.
- **Family/Drama:** Parent and child want different futures; siblings fight over inheritance.

Pro Tips & Troubleshooting

Pro Tip: Every character should enter a scene wanting something, even if it's just to avoid embarrassment or keep a secret. The more those wants clash, the higher the tension.

Troubleshooting:

- If a scene feels flat, clarify what each character wants and how those goals conflict.
- If power never shifts, find a moment for the "underdog" to gain leverage or for the dominant character to falter.

Mini Checklist

- ☐ Does each character have a clear goal in the scene?
- ☐ Are those goals in direct or subtle conflict?
- ☐ Does the balance of power shift at least once?
- ☐ Are there moments where a reveal, threat, or action changes who's in control?

Advanced Applications

- **Three-Way Conflict:** Add a third character with their own agenda. Watch the tension multiply.
- **Reversal:** Let the expected winner lose, or the

underdog win, through cleverness or luck.

- **Unresolved Tension:** End the scene with the conflict unresolved, setting up future fireworks.

Common Problems

Q: What if my scene feels like a stalemate?
A: Break the deadlock with an outside force - a phone call, new information, or an emotional outburst.

Q: How do I avoid melodrama?
A: Ground the conflict in real desires and fears, not just shouting or big gestures.

Try This

- Write a scene where two characters want opposite things and refuse to compromise. Let the power shift at least twice.
- List the goals of every character in your current chapter. Where do they align, and where do they clash?

Setting & Atmosphere

Tension isn't just about what happens between characters. It's also about where and how it happens. Setting and atmosphere can turn an ordinary scene into a nail-biter or a moment of quiet dread. A stormy night, a crowded subway, a silent hospital corridor... These details amplify emotion, hint at danger, and keep readers on edge.

Techniques in Action

1. Environmental Pressure:
- Use the physical environment to create discomfort or obstacles.
  Example: Two characters argue in a cramped elevator as the power flickers.

2. Sensory Details:
- Sights, sounds, smells, and textures can all add to the mood.
  Example: The smell of rain, the tick of a clock, the flicker of a dying light.

3. Weather & Time of Day:
- Storms, darkness, heatwaves, or sudden cold can heighten tension.
  Example: A secret meeting in a deserted park at midnight feels riskier than in broad daylight.

4. Crowds & Isolation:
- A character trapped in a crowd may feel panicked; alone, they may feel watched or vulnerable.
  Example: A protagonist flees through a festival, blending in but always looking over their shoulder.

5. Symbolic Setting:
- The setting reflects or contrasts with the

character's emotional state.

Example: A joyous wedding in a crumbling mansion, a tense family dinner in a spotless kitchen.

Genre Applications

- **Thriller:** Chase scenes through dark alleys, abandoned warehouses, or stormy roads.
- **Horror:** Haunted houses, foggy forests, empty playgrounds at night.
- **Romance:** Rain-soaked confessions, cozy cafes, or candlelit dinners with underlying tension.
- **Contemporary/Literary:** Ordinary places made extraordinary by what's at stake (a grocery store, a school hallway).

Pro Tips & Troubleshooting

Pro Tip: Let the setting interact with your characters. Make them cold, wet, or lost. The more they react to their environment, the more immersive (and tense) the scene becomes.

Troubleshooting:

- If a scene feels static, change the setting or add environmental obstacles.
- If tension drops, use weather, sound, or lighting to raise the stakes.

Mini Checklist

- ☐ Does the setting amplify the mood or stakes of the scene?
- ☐ Are sensory details (sight, sound, smell, touch, taste) used to build atmosphere?
- ☐ Does the environment create obstacles, discomfort, or urgency?
- ☐ Can you heighten tension by making the setting unfamiliar, symbolic, or threatening?

Advanced Applications

- **Contrast:** Set a tense conversation in a peaceful, beautiful place for extra dissonance.
- **Moving Setting:** Let the environment change during the scene (a storm rolls in, the sun sets, the crowd grows).
- **Symbolism:** Use objects or locations as recurring symbols of threat, hope, or change.

Common Problems

Q: What if setting details slow down the action?
A: Weave them into character action and dialogue. Show, don't tell, and keep the pace moving.

Q: How do I avoid cliché settings (dark alley, thunderstorm)?
A: Put a fresh spin on familiar places. Add unique details, or use setting to subvert expectations.

Try This

- Rewrite a key scene in a dramatically different setting. How does the change affect the tension?
- List three ways your story's environment could make life harder for your protagonist (i.e. weather, crowds, darkness, or something else).

Pacing: Sentence & Scene Structure for Tension

Pacing is the rhythm of your story; the speed at which events unfold and information is revealed. Manipulating pacing at the sentence, paragraph, and scene level can ratchet up tension, slow down emotional moments, or create a breathless rush to the climax. Mastering pacing means knowing when to linger and when to sprint.

Techniques in Action

1. Short, Sharp Sentences:
- Rapid-fire sentences and fragments speed up the pace and heighten urgency.
  Example: He ran. Heart pounding. Sirens. Closer now. He turned the corner and crashed into darkness.

2. Long, Winding Paragraphs:
- Slow the pace with detailed description, introspection, or drawn-out action to build suspense or dread.
  Example: She crept down the hallway, each step echoing in the silence, her breath loud in her ears. Shadows shifted along the walls, and the door at the end seemed impossibly far away.

3. Scene Length & Cuts:
- Short scenes, quick cuts, and abrupt transitions keep readers off balance and on edge.
- Lingering in a tense moment can stretch anticipation until it's almost unbearable.

4. Paragraph Breaks & White Space:
- Use white space to create pauses, signal a shift, or let important lines land with impact.
  Example: The phone rang. She didn't answer.

5. Cliffhangers & Scene Endings:

- End scenes on a question, a threat, or a moment of uncertainty to propel readers forward.

Genre Applications

- **Thriller:** Fast-paced action, short scenes, and cliffhanger endings.
- **Horror:** Slow, creeping dread punctuated by sudden shocks.
- **Romance:** Slow build-ups to emotional confession, then a rush of action after a turning point.
- **Literary:** Varied pacing to match the emotional arc—linger in heartbreak, speed up in crisis.

Pro Tips & Troubleshooting

Pro Tip: Read your work aloud. If a tense scene drags, try shorter sentences and tighter paragraphs. If a big reveal comes too quickly, slow down and let the tension simmer.

Troubleshooting:

- If readers skim, your pacing may be too fast. Add detail or emotional beats.
- If scenes feel slow, cut unnecessary description or internal monologue.

Mini Checklist

- ☐ Does the pacing match the tension level of the scene?
- ☐ Are sentence and paragraph lengths varied for effect?
- ☐ Do scene endings create anticipation for what's next?
- ☐ Is white space used to signal pauses, shifts, or impact?

Advanced Applications

- **Pacing Swings:** Alternate between fast and slow scenes to control reader tension and release.
- **Delayed Action:** Slow down right before a major event to maximize suspense.
- **Sentence Rhythm:** Use repetition, alliteration, or abrupt stops to mirror a character's emotional state.

Common Problems

Q: What if my climax feels rushed?

A: Slow down at key moments. Let the reader feel every beat, every decision, every consequence.

Q: How do I avoid monotony?

A: Mix up scene lengths, sentence structures, and transitions to keep the reader engaged.

Try This

- Take a tense scene and rewrite it with half the word count—focus on action and short sentences.
- Now, rewrite it again with double the length, adding sensory detail and internal thought. Which version creates more tension, and why?

Genre-Specific Tension Tips

Every genre delivers tension in its own unique way. Knowing what readers expect and how to subvert or satisfy those expectations lets you craft scenes that keep them hooked, no matter what you write.

Romance

- **Longing & Near-Misses:** Draw out confessions and keep lovers apart with misunderstandings or outside obstacles.
- **Emotional Push-Pull:** Alternate intimacy and distance, hope and heartbreak.
- **Secrets:** Hidden feelings or past mistakes threaten to surface.
- **Physical Tension:** Use touch, glances, and proximity to spark electricity.

Mystery/Thriller

- **Ticking Clocks:** Deadlines, races, and threats that get closer with every page.
- **Layered Clues:** Each answer raises new questions or reveals deeper danger.
- **Shifting Suspicions:** Trust no one. Let alliances and motives change.
- **Personal Stakes:** The case threatens something the protagonist values deeply.

Horror

- **Atmosphere:** Weather, darkness, and isolation create unease.
- **Uncertainty:** Readers question what's real, what's imagined, and who's safe.
- **Escalation:** Scares and threats get worse. Never let the pressure drop.
- **Psychological Fear:** Use guilt, shame, or dread as well as external threats.

Fantasy

- **Epic Stakes:** World-altering threats and prophecies hang over every choice.
- **Power Struggles:** Magical duels, rival factions, or forbidden knowledge.
- **Secrets:** Hidden lineages, lost spells, or ancient curses.
- **Exotic Settings:** Dangerous places force characters out of their comfort zones.

Science Fiction

- **Technological Threats:** AI, surveillance, or inventions gone wrong.
- **Ethical Dilemmas:** Progress vs. humanity, freedom vs. control.
- **Unknown Worlds:** Alien environments create constant risk and surprise.
- **Countdowns:** Races against time, oxygen, or system failure.

Historical Fiction

- **Societal Pressure:** Duty, tradition, and reputation at odds with personal desire.
- **Secrets & Scandals:** Hidden relationships or forbidden actions.
- **Public vs. Private Stakes:** Choices have consequences for family, community, or nation.
- **Imminent Upheaval:** War, revolution, or disaster looms.

Contemporary/Literary

- **Relational Tension:** Family secrets, betrayals, and shifting power dynamics.
- **Small Moments, Big Stakes:** Everyday decisions with outsized emotional impact.
- **Subtext & Silence:** What's left unsaid is

often most powerful.

- **Personal Deadlines:** Milestones, moves, or losses force decisions.

Young Adult

- **Identity & Belonging:** Fitting in, breaking out, or forging a new path.
- **Peer Pressure:** Friends, rivals, and first loves test loyalties.
- **Secrets:** Hiding the truth from adults, friends, or oneself.
- **Firsts:** First love, first betrayal, first failure; every emotion is heightened.

Women's Fiction

- **Balancing Acts:** Juggling personal dreams with family or societal roles.
- **Friendship & Family:** Bonds tested by secrets, change, or time.
- **Internal Conflict:** Choosing self over others, or vice versa.
- **Second Chances:** Reinvention, forgiveness, or starting over.

Paranormal/Urban Fantasy

- **Hidden Worlds:** Danger and magic beneath the surface of everyday life.
- **Power & Cost:** Using abilities comes with risk or sacrifice.
- **Secrets:** Concealed identities, forbidden alliances, or supernatural threats.
- **Collision of Realms:** Tension between human and paranormal communities.

Mini Checklist

- ☐ Am I using the tension techniques readers expect for my genre?
- ☐ Are personal, relational, and external stakes layered throughout?
- ☐ Do scenes end with a hook, twist, or unresolved question?
- ☐ Are my characters' wants, fears, and secrets driving the tension?

Common Pitfalls & How to Fix Them

Even experienced writers can accidentally deflate tension. Recognizing these common missteps and knowing how to fix them keeps your story sharp, engaging, and unputdownable.

Pitfall 1: Over-Explaining or Info-Dumping

What Happens:

You reveal too much, too soon, or slow the story with backstory, explanations, or worldbuilding.

How to Fix:

- Reveal information on a need-to-know basis. Let readers wonder and discover alongside the characters.
- Replace exposition with action, dialogue, or discovery.
- Use subtext: let what's unsaid be just as important as what's revealed.

Example:

Instead of telling readers all about a character's tragic past, show how they flinch at a certain name or avoid a familiar street.

Pitfall 2: Tension Drop-Offs

What Happens:

After a big reveal, scare, or argument, the story loses momentum (characters relax too soon, or the stakes disappear).

How to Fix:

- After a reveal, immediately introduce a new question, complication, or risk.
- Layer tension. Let one problem be solved, but another emerge.
- Use pacing to your advantage: a brief lull can work, but only if it's the calm before a bigger

storm.

Example:
After the villain is unmasked, the real threat is revealed: they weren't working alone.

Pitfall 3: Telegraphing Twists

What Happens:
You drop heavy hints or foreshadowing that makes plot twists predictable.

How to Fix:
- Be subtle. Less is more. Trust readers to pick up on small clues.
- Use misdirection: distract with a red herring or a subplot.
- Save the biggest surprises for when readers (and characters) least expect them.

Example:
If everyone suspects one character is the traitor, make the twist about someone else, or about why the suspicion exists.

Pitfall 4: Flat Dialogue & On-the-Nose Writing

What Happens:
Characters say exactly what they mean, and every conversation resolves cleanly.

How to Fix:
- Add subtext, secrets, and misunderstandings.
- Let dialogue be messy. Include interruptions, unfinished thoughts, and hidden motives.
- Use body language and silence to layer meaning.

Example:
Instead of "I'm angry with you," try "Don't wait up," with a slammed door.

Pitfall 5: Stakes That Don't Escalate

What Happens:

Every scene feels the same; no sense of rising danger or urgency.

How to Fix:

- Make each obstacle harder than the last.
- Raise the cost of failure. What do characters stand to lose now that they didn't before?
- Combine internal and external stakes for more complexity.

Example:

A lost job isn't just about money. It threatens a character's self-worth, relationships, and future.

Troubleshooting Checklist

- ☐ Am I revealing too much, too soon?
- ☐ Does every scene have something at stake (emotionally, physically, or relationally)?
- ☐ Are there moments when tension drops? Can I add a new question or risk?
- ☐ Do I trust my readers to pick up on subtle clues, or am I spelling everything out?
- ☐ Are twists and reveals truly surprising, but still earned?

Quick Fixes

- If a scene feels slow, cut the explanation and add an unanswered question.
- If tension drops after a reveal, introduce a new complication right away.
- If dialogue is flat, rewrite with more subtext, interruption, or body language.
- If stakes feel low, ask: "What's the worst thing that could happen now?"

Tension Audit Checklist

Even the best stories can lose tension without warning. Use this audit before, during, or after drafting to spot weak spots and instantly identify where tension can be raised. This tool works for any genre, any scene.

Tension Audit: Scene-by-Scene

For each scene or chapter, ask:

- ☐ Is there something the reader or character doesn't know yet?
- ☐ Are at least two characters' goals in conflict (even subtly)?
- ☐ Is there a deadline, countdown, or time pressure?
- ☐ Are there secrets, lies, or hidden motives at play?
- ☐ Does the setting add discomfort, danger, or unease?
- ☐ Is body language or subtext used to deepen tension?
- ☐ Does the pacing match the level of tension needed (fast for action, slow for dread)?
- ☐ Are the stakes clear, personal, and escalating?
- ☐ Does the scene end with a hook, question, or unresolved issue?
- ☐ If tension drops, is another source of tension introduced right away?

How to Use This Checklist

- Run through the list as you draft or revise each scene.
- If you answer "no" to several questions, pick one or two techniques to add.
- Don't force every technique into every

scene—but aim to keep tension alive on every page.

Pro Tip: *Keep a printed copy of this checklist at your desk, or paste it at the top of your manuscript as a reminder. The more you use it, the more instinctive tension-building will become.*

Next Steps

Tension is what keeps readers glued to your story - eager, anxious, and desperate to know what happens next. By mastering these techniques, you have the power to turn even the quietest scene into a page-turner and make every chapter unforgettable.

Remember:

- Layer tension through unanswered questions, time pressure, subtext, and setting.
- Let your characters' conflicting goals and shifting power keep things unpredictable.
- Use pacing and genre-specific tricks to keep your readers on the edge of their seats.

Don't be afraid to experiment. Try new techniques, combine them in surprising ways, and always trust your instincts. The more you practice, the sharper your sense of tension will become.

Keep this guide nearby as you draft and revise. Whenever a scene feels flat, flip back, choose a technique, and watch your story come alive.

About The Author

Connie Bauldree is a self-published author with a passion for storytelling and helping others craft their own. Writing under the pen names Connie Connolly, Emersyn Kane, Payton Rome, and Connie Bauldree, she has authored over 75 non-fiction writing resources and published nine fiction novels spanning multiple genres.

Connie is the owner of Author by Design, the creative hub behind the Builder Series and the Writer's Block Box, resources designed to inspire and empower writers at every stage of their journey. She is also the co-founder of SisterScribe Academy, a platform dedicated to supporting and educating aspiring authors.

Connie believes every writer has a story worth telling and is passionate about providing the tools and frameworks to help them succeed.

When she's not writing or developing innovative tools for authors, Connie enjoys connecting with her audience on social media. Follow her @authorbydesign for tips, updates, and inspiration.

Stay in touch and explore her offerings by signing up for her newsletter at www.authorbydesign.co. or www.writersblockboxes.com.